PHOTOGRAPHY

Published by Smart Apple Media
123 South Broad Street
Mankato, Minnesota 56001

Photos: page 8–CORBIS; page 11–CORBIS/David Lees;
page 13–CORBIS/Hulton-Deutsch Collection;
page 15– CORBIS/ Paul Almasy;
page 23–CORBIS/ Hulton-Deutsch Collection

Design and Production: EvansDay Design

Library of Congress Cataloging-in-Publication Data
Vander Hook, Sue, 1949–
Photography / by Sue Vander Hook
p. cm. – (Making contact)
Includes index.
Summary: Surveys the history and development
of photography, from experiments with light in
ancient China to the modern computer age.
ISBN 1-887068-62-7
1. Photography—History—Juvenile literature.
[1. Photography—History.] I. Title. II. Series:
Making contact (Mankato, Minn.)

TR15.V36   1999
770—dc21   98-20887

First edition

9 8 7 6 5 4 3 2 1

M6817

PHOTOGRAPHY

MAKING CONTACT

SUE VANDER HOOK

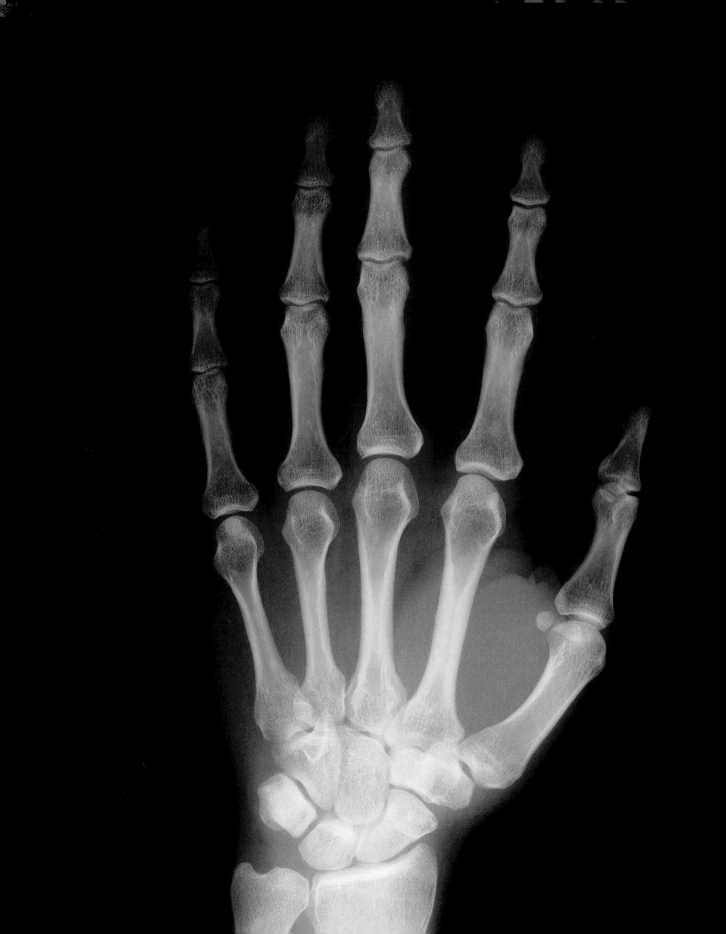

FOR THOUSANDS OF YEARS, PEOPLE have created images to help them remember important events in their lives. Prehistoric people scratched pictures into rocks and painted images on cave walls. Many of these early artistic creations still exist. But it wasn't until the early 19th century that true-to-life images could be captured and preserved. Over the years, **photography** has led to milestone achievements in science, medicine, and entertainment. It has also given us a way to record history and our way of life.

Writing With Light

The word "photography" comes from two ancient Greek words: *photos,* meaning "light," and *grapho,* meaning "writing." Photography, then, is "writing with light." Anyone who has worn a bathing suit for a few hours in bright summer sunshine has personally experienced the principles of photography. Sunlight

will darken the exposed, light-sensitive skin, while the skin covered by the bathing suit will remain light. This is the basis of photography: an object is exposed to light, and an image of the object is captured on light-sensitive material.

Chinese and Greek scholars began experimenting with light thousands of years ago. In the fourth century B.C., the Greek philosopher Aristotle discovered a way to watch a partial **eclipse** of the sun without harming his eyes. He learned that a tiny pinhole punched in a thin sheet of paper or cloth will funnel light into a cone-shaped image. By funneling sunlight through this tiny hole and onto a wall, he was able to witness the eclipse. Aristotle's technique had used light

In the middle of the 19th century, some people went on special trips just to take photographs. They took pictures of the wonders of the world and printed them in books. These photographs allowed people to "travel" around the world simply by looking at pictures.

7

* TINY IMAGES OF A SOLAR ECLIPSE FORMED BY SUNLIGHT SHI

to create an image. But it was only a temporary one that lasted as long as he held up the pinhole. Hundreds of years would pass before anyone would be able to capture an image and preserve it on a surface.

In the late 16th century, almost 2,000 years after Aristotle, a man named Giovanni Battista del la Porta stunned an Italian audience by presenting a mysterious image on a wall. Del la Porta belonged to the Academy of Secrets—a group of scientists who explored revolutionary ideas and experiments. After being seated in a darkened room called a **camera obscura**, the audience watched as fascinating, upside-down

8

✳ AN ILLUSTRATION SHOWING HOW THE CAMERA OBSCURA TECHNIQUE WORKED.

pictures came alive on the wall. What the amazed audience didn't know was that there was a pinhole in the wall across the room. On the other side of the wall were actors who had been paid to frolic around; their antics were projected by light through the pinhole and onto the facing wall. Like Aristotle, del la Porta had captured an image with light. Members of the audience, astounded by the strange show, suspected him of black magic.

More than 100 years later, people were still using the camera

The Reverend Charles Dodgson, better known as the famous author Lewis Carroll, took up photography as a hobby in 1856. Little girls in fancy dresses were his favorite subjects. His most famous photograph was of Alice Liddell; she became the title character in his fanciful book, *Alice in Wonderland*.

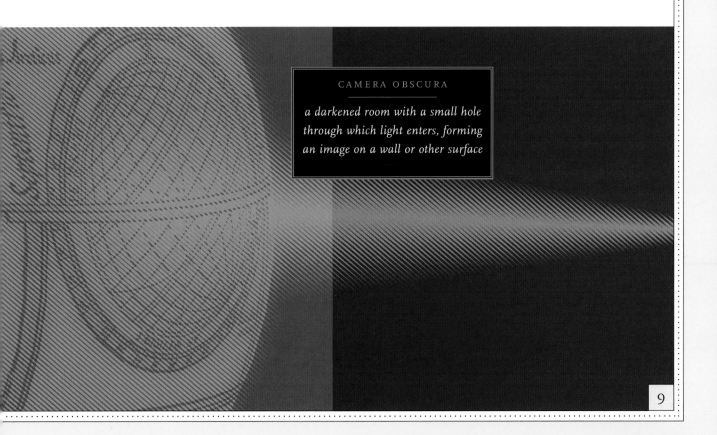

CAMERA OBSCURA

a darkened room with a small hole through which light enters, forming an image on a wall or other surface

obscura, adding mirrors to reflect the images right side up. Many artists had their own camera obscuras, which allowed them to make quick, accurate sketches of still objects by tracing the projected images.

In 1725, a scientist name Johann Schulze was experimenting with light. After mixing chalk and a chemical called silver nitrate in a jar, he placed stencils of letters over the top of the open jar. After light had shone into the jar for a while, Schulze discovered that the parts of the solution exposed to light turned dark, creating an image of the letters in the solution. Little did Schulze know that his experiment would pave the way for photography.

Thirty-five years later, a Frenchman named Tiphaigne de la Roche made

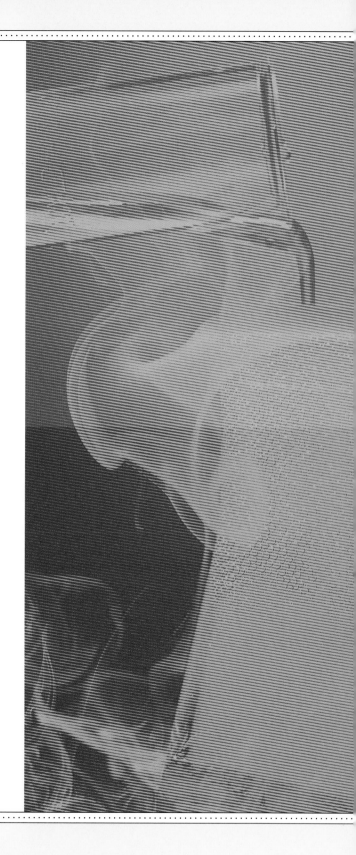

an amazing prediction. In an imaginary tale called *Giphantie*, he wrote about capturing images from nature on a canvas coated in a sticky substance. In the story, a character carries the image to a mysterious dark room. An hour later, the canvas is dry, and the image remains permanently captured on the strange surface. De la Roche's prediction would come true just a few decades after his death.

The first aerial photographs were taken by Felix Tournachon, a man known as "The Great Nadar." He took pictures of Paris from his hot air balloon, *Le Géant*, in 1863. Two weeks later, a wind blew the balloon into Germany, where it crashed, breaking Tournachon's leg.

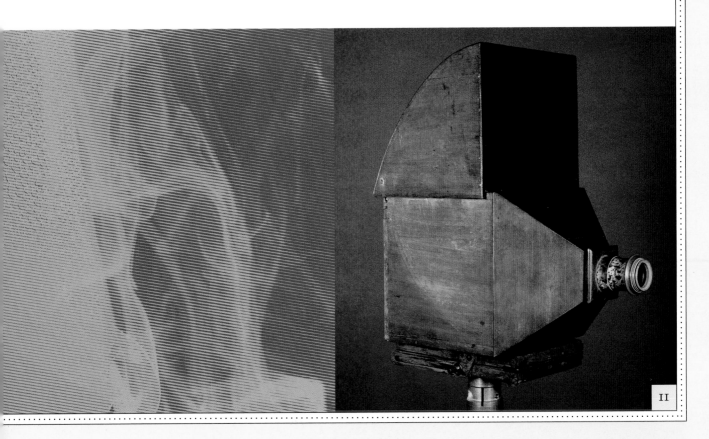

II

* FOR MORE THAN A CENTURY, THE CAMERA OBSCURA WAS USED TO CREATE MOVING IMAGES.

Capturing Images

When scientists began combining light and chemicals in the hopes of preserving images, photography was born. In the early 1800s, Thomas Wedgwood successfully captured **silhouettes** on a surface by using silver nitrate. But his silhouettes faded and eventually disappeared. No one knew how to make the image permanent.

In 1826, a Frenchman named Nicephore Niépce successfully produced a permanent image. He achieved this milestone by coating a **pewter** plate with a cement-like substance called bitumen of Judea, which hardened when exposed to light. Niépce's first image took eight hours to harden onto the **plate.** But that image, taken from an upper window of a house, became the first permanent photograph. It still exists today in a museum at the University of Texas.

Three years later, Niépce reluctantly agreed to become partners with a man named Louis Daguerre, who had also been experimenting with images. Although Niépce died just four years after the partnership was formed, Daguerre continued experimenting.

In the 1860s, soldiers in the American Civil War found the lightweight paper pictures to be a big improvement over the heavy daguerreotype plates. It was much easier to carry photographs of loved ones in their pockets when they went to battle.

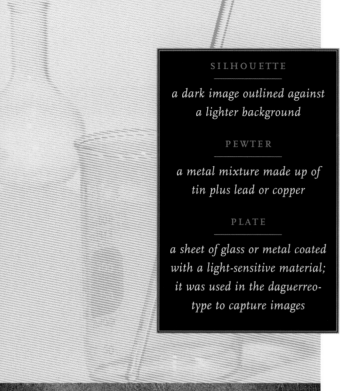

SILHOUETTE

a dark image outlined against a lighter background

PEWTER

a metal mixture made up of tin plus lead or copper

PLATE

a sheet of glass or metal coated with a light-sensitive material; it was used in the daguerreotype to capture images

He tried to convince people to invest money in his project, which he called the "daguerreotype." He eloquently insisted that "the daguerreotype is not merely an instrument which serves to draw Nature. . . . [It] gives her the power to reproduce herself."

Daguerre soon discovered a way to reduce light exposure time from eight hours to just half an hour. He also discovered that an image could be made permanent by dipping it in a salt solution. In 1839, the French government bought the rights to the daguerreotype, then offered information about it freely as a gift to the world. Within a few months, Daguerre's instruction manual had been distributed around the world in a dozen languages.

✳ LOUIS DAGUERRE, WHO DEVELOPED ONE OF THE FIRST METHODS OF CAPTURING LIFELIKE IMAGES.

The daguerreotype was fairly easy to create. The plate, which was made of copper and coated with a silver solution, was placed in a large dark box, or camera. The plate was then exposed to light—which entered through a tiny hole—for a considerable amount of time. This meant that the people who were being photographed had to sit very still for a long time as well. After exposure, the plate was taken to a dark room for development. There, it was heated over a container of pure **mercury**. The picture was made permanent by repeatedly pouring a soda solution over the plate; this removed

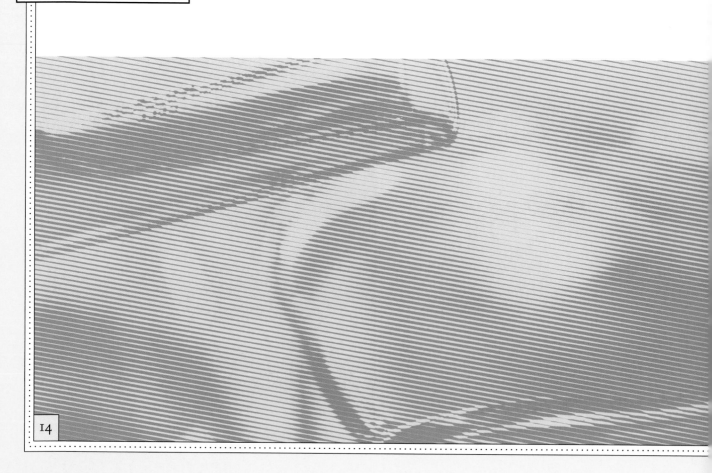

any extra silver. Finally, the plate was covered with a thin layer of gold and protected by a piece of glass.

People heard that creating a daguerreotype did not require artistic ability or knowledge of drawing; it was said that anyone could become as accomplished at image-making as the inventor. With such publicity, Daguerre's system of photography quickly became a worldwide success.

MERCURY

a heavy, silver-white metallic element that is liquid at normal temperatures

✳ A DAGUERREOTYPE CAMERA MADE IN 1839, THE YEAR THE DEVICE BEGAN SPREADING WORLDWIDE.

Americans were especially excited about the daguerreotype. The United States had a head start on photography thanks to painter and inventor Samuel Morse. While Morse was in Paris demonstrating his new invention, a communications device called the telegraph, he exchanged secrets with Daguerre and brought the daguerreotype back to the U.S. Morse and his partner, John Draper, began experimenting with the new process, and Morse demonstrated his

own version of the daguerreotype just two months after France offered the idea to the world. A few months later, Draper made a successful portrait of his sister Dorothy. This picture, which needed only 65 seconds of exposure time, is one of the earliest surviving examples of photography.

The daguerreotype was popular, but it did have some serious limitations. The pictures were small—usually two by three inches (5 by 7.5 cm)—but they were also heavy since they were developed on metal. They had a fragile surface that required a protective glass cover and a large frame or case. And each picture

Around 1900, the Chicago & Alton Railroad hired George R. Lawrence to take a picture of a new luxury train. To do this, Lawrence made the "Mammoth," a giant camera weighing seven tons (6.4 t). It took 15 men and 10 gallons (38 L) of chemicals to make one huge print.

* AN EARLY DAGUERREOTYPE PORTRAIT OF A MOTHER AND CHILD.

was a one-of-a-kind original that could not be duplicated; there was no **negative** from which copies could be made.

By 1843, an entire photo industry had emerged in the United States. For the first time in history, people who were not wealthy could afford to own portraits. A person's photographic portrait, called a *phiz*, could be purchased at a cost of two to five dollars. People opened portrait studios and big-city galleries. Individuals with daguerreotypes traveled throughout the country, giving paying customers the chance to have their pictures taken.

Technology developed rapidly. Soon, newspapers were able to copy and print pictures. One early group of such pictures showed miners working in gold fields during the Cal-

NEGATIVE

an image in which the light and dark tones are reversed

ifornia gold rush. Publishers began printing books that contained pictures of the world's great wonders, and magazines printed a variety of pictures that included farms, churches, people, and nature. By 1851, pictures needed only two or three seconds of exposure time, and by the mid-1850s, photography had become commonplace in the United States.

While the daguerreotype business was growing quickly in America, an English inventor named William Fox Talbot began using negatives. Talbot produced paper negatives called *calotypes*,

The pigeon camera was invented in 1907 by the son of a pharmacist, who used pigeons to deliver medicine from their store to a hospital in the mountains. One day, he decided to attach a miniature camera to a bird. An automatic device in the camera snapped an aerial picture every 30 seconds.

19

✳ As cameras improved in the late 1800s, almost anyone could be a photographer.

from which he could make many paper prints of the same picture. Because of his invention, Talbot claimed to be the founder of modern photography. But he did not give his idea to the world for free; instead, he received a **patent** for his invention. Although Talbot tried to sell **licenses** for the right to use his negatives, people didn't want to pay for his process when they could use the daguerreotype for free. It would take two decades' worth of new inventions to bring about the widespread use of negatives.

In the 1920s, reporters competed fiercely for front-page stories. Although cameras were not allowed at executions, Tom Howard, a reporter for the *New York Daily News*, was able to get the first picture of an electric-chair execution by strapping a small camera to his ankle.

PATENT

*an official government docu-
ment giving an inventor the
exclusive right to make, use,
and sell an invention for a
certain number of years*

LICENSE

*formal permission from
an authority to do a
specific thing*

THE MAN
BEHIND
THE GUN.

21

* PHOTOGRAPHY HAS PLAYED A CRITICAL ROLE IN PRESERVING HISTORY FOR MORE THAN 150 YEARS.

George Eastman, born in New York on July 12, 1854, began his life during the period of the daguerreotype's greatest popularity. During Eastman's lifetime, science and technology merged to create many new things—automobiles, X rays, light bulbs, skyscrapers, and others. As a teenager, Eastman earned money as a messenger

for an insurance company. Five years later, he became a junior clerk at a bank.

When Eastman was 24, he planned a vacation. Friends encouraged him to take pictures of his trip, so he gathered all the proper equipment, including a camera as big as a microwave oven. He purchased a tent so he could prepare plates before exposure and then develop the wet plates in the tent before they dried out. Eastman also bought chemicals, glass tanks, a heavy plate holder, and a big jug for water. When he was finished buying supplies, Eastman described his photographic equipment as "a pack-horse load."

Eastman never took the planned vacation, but he did become very interested in photography. He wanted to make the process

> During World War II, Kodak manufactured a spy camera that looked almost exactly like a small matchbox. A secret agent could snap a picture just by pressing a tiny button.

much easier and less expensive, and he soon did. After reading about a dry plate process in a British magazine, Eastman began trying to improve photographic methods, working at the bank during the day and experimenting in his mother's kitchen at night.

After much work, Eastman patented his own dry plate process. He also created a machine that could prepare large numbers of plates. Eastman soon decided to sell dry plates to other photographers, and in 1880, he started a business called the Eastman Company. It became more than a place where dry plates were made; as

23

* GEORGE EASTMAN, WHOSE KODAK CAMERAS MADE PHOTOGRAPHY AVAILABLE TO EVERYONE.

Eastman described it, his business began "to make the camera as convenient as the pencil."

Eastman's first accomplishment was loading photographic paper on a roll holder. This wonderful innovation let people take many pictures and develop them later instead of having to develop each plate immediately after taking the picture.

By 1885, Eastman was advertising a new material called film to be used in place of paper. His film had the same kind of light-sensitive, silver-salt coating as paper, but it could be rolled tightly around a spool. Enough film could fit in a camera to take dozens of photographs before reloading. The film also provided a much clearer image than paper.

Scientists used a special camera to study atomic weapons in the early days of atomic research. This camera could photograph one-millionth of a second of an atomic explosion, capturing an image of the early stage of an atomic fireball.

✳ BY THE EARLY 20TH CENTURY, NEWSPAPERS AND OTHER MEDIA RELIED HEAVILY ON PHOTOGRAPHS.

To Eastman's disappointment, few photographers used his new film. He decided that if his business was to prosper, he would have to reach the general public; to do this, he created the name "Kodak" for his products. Since Eastman had always been fond of the letter "k," he made up a name that started and ended with the letter. The first Kodak products were advertised in newspapers and magazines in ads written by Eastman himself. By 1888, he was advertising the

✳ THE BROWNIE, AN EASY-TO-USE KODAK CAMERA THAT COST JUST ONE DOLLAR IN 1900.

Kodak camera with the slogan, "You push the button, we do the rest." The days of the pack-horse load of photography equipment were over.

Eastman believed that photography should be available at a price that everyone could afford. By 1896, the Eastman Company had made 100,000 Kodak cameras and was manufacturing about 400 miles (667 km) of film each month. At the time, the camera sold for five dollars, but Eastman still wasn't satisfied; he wanted to make a camera that would sell for just one dollar. He succeeded in 1900 by designing a small camera called the Brownie. Eastman had at last accomplished both his goals: he had given the world an inexpensive, handheld camera, and he had simplified photography to little more than pressing a button.

By the middle of the 20th century, the camera had become a common piece of equipment with a range of uses. Photographers had become artists. People everywhere were busy taking portraits, photographing nature, and capturing history on film. By this time, scientists had discovered how to photograph

the inside of a human body using X rays—a great breakthrough in medicine. Thomas Edison had developed the motion picture camera, which would revolutionize news coverage and entertainment. Color photographs had become a reality. Banks and libraries had begun using **microfilm**, a technology that let them copy and store printed material in a tiny amount of space.

The second half of the 20th century took photography to all walks of life. In the 1950s, people began using low-priced home movie cameras to capture family memories. They could project color slides on screens or living room walls. Office workers took pictures of important documents on machines called photocopiers. Divers used

In 1989, Kodak introduced its single-use camera, sometimes called a disposable or throwaway camera. This product became popular with travelers and people who would forget to bring their camera to special events.

underwater cameras to explore the bottom of the ocean, and the related technology of **sonar** used bouncing sound waves to capture images of underwater objects.

In 1962, John Glenn became the first American astronaut to orbit the earth. A special camera recorded his journey through space at 17,400 miles (29,000 km) per hour. Another camera accompanied astronauts Edwin "Buzz" Aldrin and Neil Armstrong in 1969 when they became the first people to walk on the moon. Amazing photographs of the moon's surface brought home the reality of a far-off place that people had been curious about for centuries.

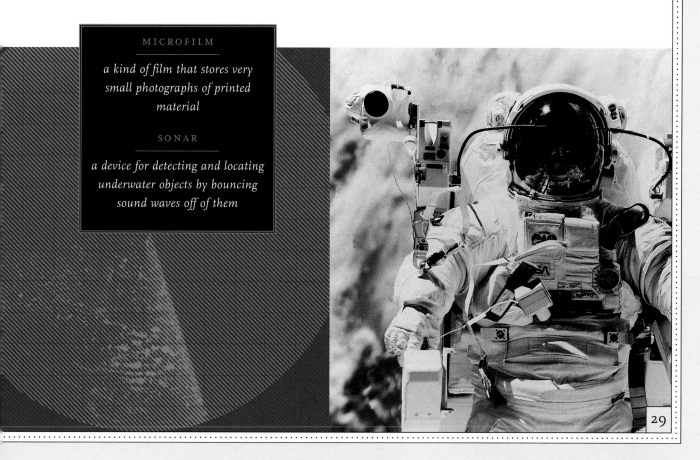

MICROFILM

a kind of film that stores very small photographs of printed material

SONAR

a device for detecting and locating underwater objects by bouncing sound waves off of them

29

✳ FOR YEARS, PHOTOGRAPHY HAS ENABLED US TO SEE WHAT LIES BEYOND EARTH'S ATMOSPHERE.

Whether through X rays that explore the innermost parts of the body or through images from the outer limits of space, photography has taken us on an incredible journey. The 1990s have taken this journey of discovery even farther by merging photography with the computer age. People can now use digital cameras to take pictures in a format that computers can understand. The cameras take pictures made up of microscopic sections called **pixels**. Each pixel receives a number code. Computers can read this **digital** code and translate it into an image on the screen.

Today, a computer can also change or improve a photographic image by making it sharper or eliminating unwanted parts of the picture. Computers can combine several images into a new image or add artistic effects and textures. In fact, a computer can alter colors and details one pixel at a time, creating a photographed subject that only appears to be real.

Computer users can now see colorful images from around the world on the **Internet**, a system made possible by laser beams that send digital codes through telephone wires. Newspapers and television newsrooms use this technology

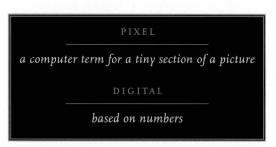

PIXEL

a computer term for a tiny section of a picture

DIGITAL

based on numbers

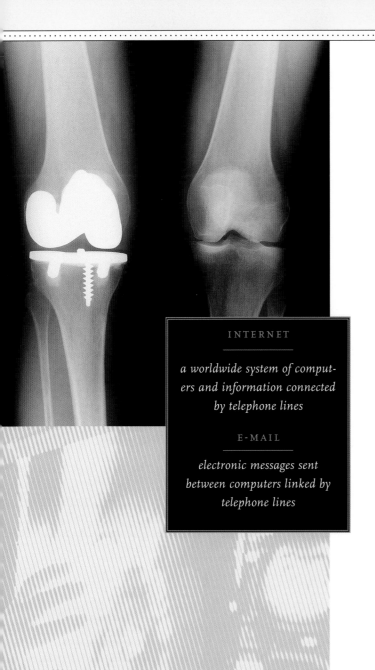

INTERNET

a worldwide system of computers and information connected by telephone lines

E-MAIL

electronic messages sent between computers linked by telephone lines

to receive photographs a few seconds after they are taken. Hospitals send medical images on phone lines to other hospitals. Many people use computers as electronic photo albums; they can share their photos with others by displaying them on the Internet or by attaching the images to **e-mail**.

It's difficult to predict where photography will take us next. The journey began with the simple image of an eclipse seen through a small pinhole. It has taken us to places of beauty, recorded a pictorial history of the last century, and brought amazing improvements to science and medicine. But for most people, the best thing about photography is perhaps its most basic role: it helps us remember the important events of our lives.

✳ X RAYS, ONE OF THE MOST IMPORTANT DEVELOPMENTS IN THE HISTORY OF MEDICINE.

A
Academy of Secrets 8
aerial photography 19
Aldrin, Edwin "Buzz" 29
Alice in Wonderland 9
Aristotle 6, 8
Armstrong, Neil 29

C
calotypes 19
camera obscura 8–10, 11
cameras
 Brownie 26, 27
 digital 30
 Kookie Kamera 14
 (the) "Mammoth" 16
 motion picture 28
 pigeon 19
 Polaroid 26
 Polaroid-Land 26
 single-use 28
 underwater 28–29
color photography 26

D
Daguerre, Louis 12–13, 15, 16
daguerreotypes 12, 13–15, 20
de la Roche, Tiphaigne 10–11
del la Porta, Giovanni Battista 8–9
Dodgson, Charles 9
Draper, John 16
dry plate process 23–24

E
Eastman Company 23–24, 27
Eastman, George 22–24, 27
Edison, Thomas 28

F
film 24

G
Giphantie 11
Glenn, John 29

I
Internet 30, 31

K
Kodak 22, 26–27, 28

L
Land, Edwin 26
Lawrence, George R. 16
Liddell, Alice 9

M
microfilm 28, 29
Morse, Samuel 16

N
negatives 18, 19–20
Niépce, Nicephore 12–13

P
phiz 18
photocopiers 28

S
Schulze, Johann 10
slides 28
Snow White 30

T
Talbot, William Fox 19–20
Tournachon, Felix 11

W
Wedgwood, Thomas 12

X
X rays 28, 30, 31